Stop!

Beverley Randell
Illustrated by Meredith Thomas

Look up the road.

Look down the road.

Here comes a car.

Wait.

Look up the road.

Look down the road.

Here comes a bus.

Wait.

5

Look up the road.

Look down the road.

Here comes a truck.

Wait.

7

Look up the road.

Look down the road.

Here comes a van.

Wait.

Look up the road.

Look down the road.

Here comes a bike.

Wait.

11

Look up the road.

Look down the road.

Here comes a motorcycle.

Wait.

Look up the road.

Look down the road.

We can cross now.